Contents

MW01042804

Action:
defense

For many animals, survival
depends on defense
systems that evolve from
both physical and
behavioral adaptations.
Camouflage, flight from
attack, withdrawal, threat,
and bluff, using physical
armor, and cooperation are
all strategies of the defense
systems that animals use
when defending
themselves from attack.

QUESTION:

what do you know about the
defense systems of animals?

defense systems

The Strategies

Predict: What do you think this chapter will be about?

Strategies of defense fall into different categories. These categories include:

(a) Camouflage and Mimicry

This line of defense can work before a predator starts to advance on its prey. An animal that is camouflaged is less likely to have to fight off an attack, because the chances of it having been seen for itself have been lessened.

(b) Active and Passive Action

Animals that are attacked can take active or passive action. For example, spines on a sea urchin or

defense

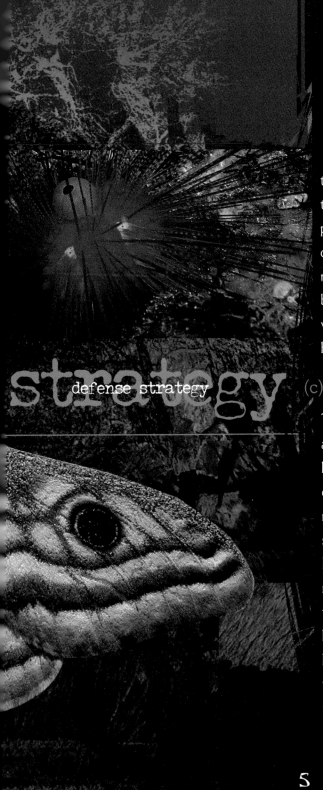

the protective shell on a tortoise are both forms of passive defense. An active defense is when an animal runs, threatens, or retaliates by attacking the predator with teeth, horns, or hooves.

(c) Group Defense Action

This line of defense involves action within family groups, herds, shoals, or whole communities where animals may cooperate in a shared strategy against predators. For example, animal herds may use defensive positions that protect members of the herd. Some insect colonies have defensive individuals whose specific task it is to protect other community members.

defense strategy

Camouflage

Predict What do you think this chapter will be about?

Many animals rely on eyesight when hunting, so some prey try to avoid being seen by camouflaging, or making their bodies blend in with the environment. Camouflage takes different forms.

Countershading is one example of camouflage. This is where an animal is darker on the upper part of its body and lighter underneath. Countershading helps an animal blend in with the background more effectively, therefore decreasing the chances of being spotted by a predator.

Disruptive coloration is another form of camouflage. This can be seen in zebras and butterfly fish. Outside their natural environment, these boldly-striped animals stand out, but within it, these striped patterns help to break up the body outline.

QUESTION:

countershadin

What meaning does the word counter bring to this term?

Compare and contrast
Countershading and disruptive coloration

Countershading	Disruptive coloration
animal is darker on upper part of body and lighter underneath	?

Camouflage mimicry is another way of escaping detection. This is where an animal mimics some feature of another part of the environment that a predator would normally consider inedible. For instance, the sphinx moth looks exactly like a woody twig. Leaf and stick insects use this mimicry, too.

They combine color and shape to look like the leaf and stem that they are clinging to. Flatfish, for example, can change color to match their background. They also flick sand over their bodies to hide their outlines on the seabed.

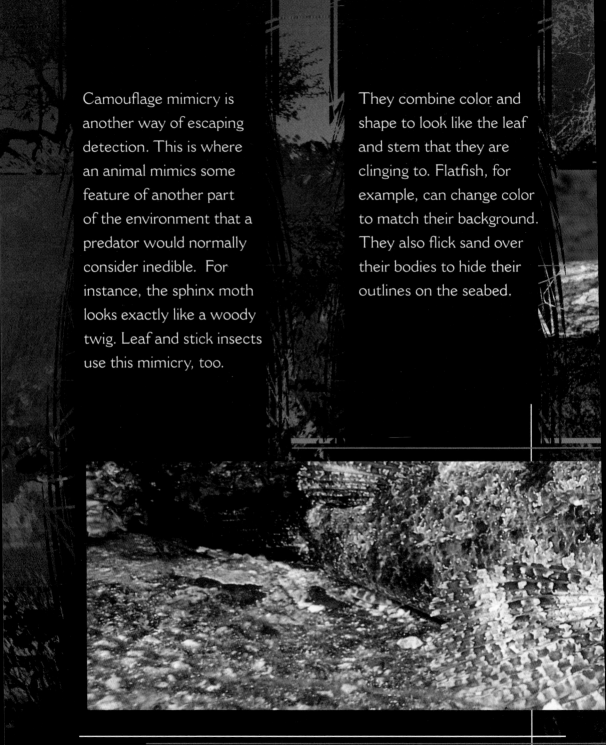

animal mimics

animal mimics

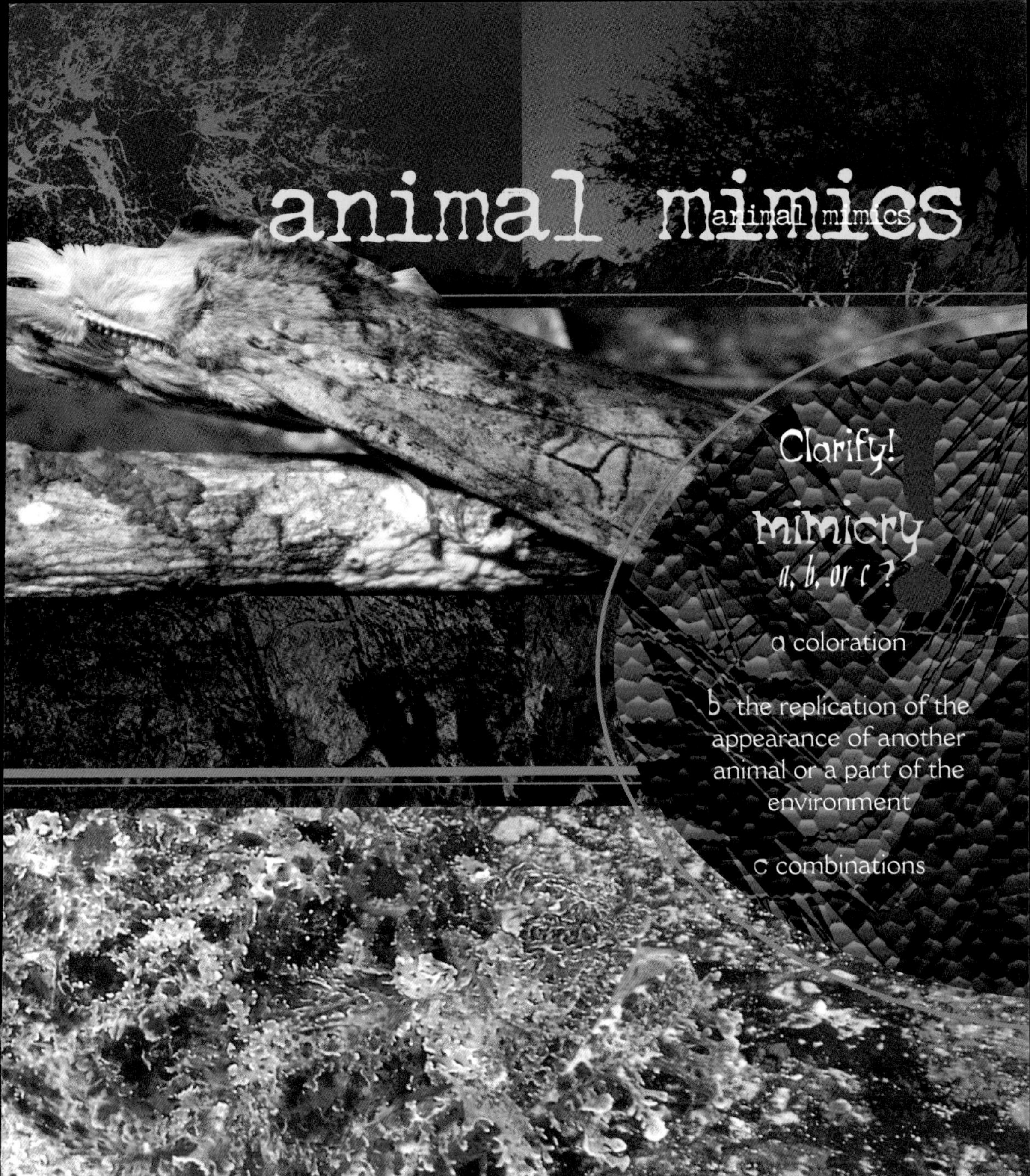

Clarify!

mimicry
a, b, or c ?

a coloration

b the replication of the appearance of another animal or a part of the environment

c combinations

Although both camouflage and camouflage mimicry is useful to an animal, one drawback is the need to remain motionless. This inevitably conflicts with the need to be active – for example, to feed. Camouflaged animals tend to resolve this problem by feeding at times (mostly at night) when predation is less likely.

QUESTION:
Which words match the term

inevitably conflicts

a assists easily

b is always at odds

remain motionless

remain motionless

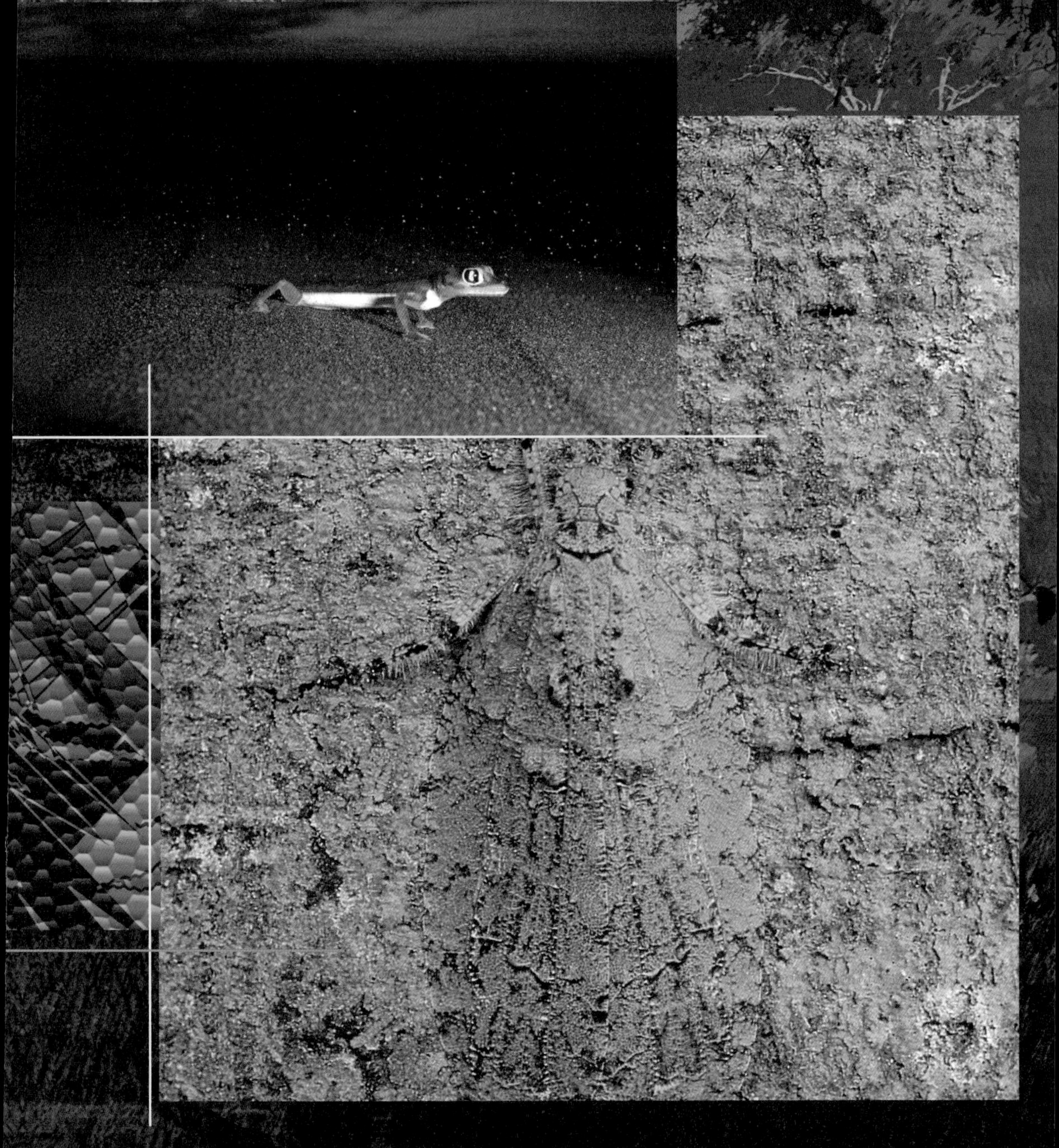

Withdrawal, Threa and Bluff

Some animals are slow-moving or immobile and have developed body protection, such as hard shells and protective spines. These animals sit tight, withdrawing or hiding vulnerable parts. For example, turtles, snails, clams, and mussels pull in the soft parts of their bodies. Hedgehogs and porcupine fish can erect their spines or roll into a ball for extra protection.

Clarify!

vulnerable
a, b, or c ?

a luscious

b exposed to attack

c hard-covered

body

protection body protection

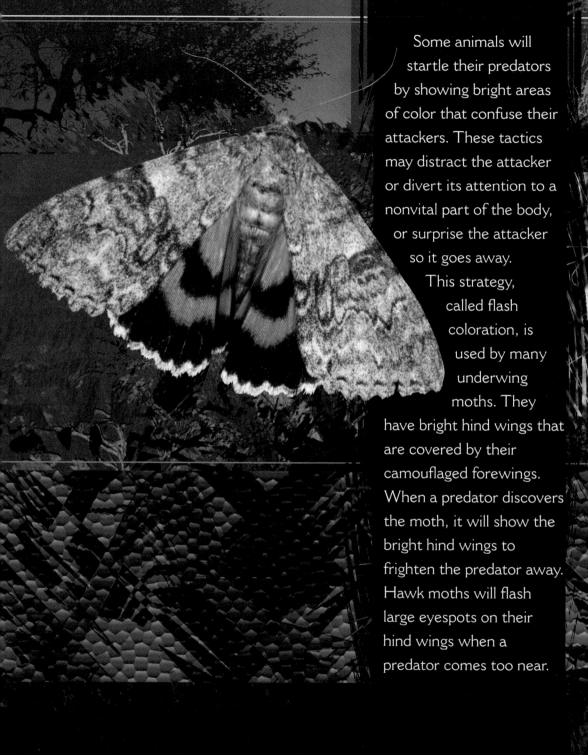

Some animals will startle their predators by showing bright areas of color that confuse their attackers. These tactics may distract the attacker or divert its attention to a nonvital part of the body, or surprise the attacker so it goes away.

This strategy, called flash coloration, is used by many underwing moths. They have bright hind wings that are covered by their camouflaged forewings. When a predator discovers the moth, it will show the bright hind wings to frighten the predator away. Hawk moths will flash large eyespots on their hind wings when a predator comes too near.

frighten the predator

Action and response chart

Action	Response
Moth flashes bright hind wings	Predator is frightened off

Find another action and response example!

Flight from

For animals that are more mobile, the first response to a predator is flight. Some animals, such as prairie dogs, will bolt to the security of their burrows. Others may attempt to outrun the pursuer.

Night-flying moths are able to detect the ultrasonic calls and slicks given out by the echolocating bat. These moths have developed evasive strategies. They hear the sounds of the bats before they are detected, but they are unable to match the speed of the bat. If the bat is close, the moth will fly erratically or close its wings and drop to the ground.

erratically
Which is the correct synonym: a, b, or c ?

a slowly

b silently

c unevenly

Attack

QUESTION: How does the zigzagging of a hare in flight prevent it from being caught?

Other animals will use erratic patterns to avoid predators. Hares will zigzag away from foxes. Antelopes use agility and speed to escape from hunters. As they run, they occasionally leap into the air with all four feet leaving the ground at the same time. This is called stotting. It confuses the enemy and may also give a message to the attacker to look for an animal that is less fit.

Synonym: A word or term that has the same meaning as another word or term

Interesting Defenses

Predict: What do you think this chapter will tell us about interesting defenses?

Sometimes when an animal is cornered, it will attempt to bluff predators by display. Toads and bullfrogs will swallow air and inflate their lungs and vocal sacs so that they look bigger than their normal size.

Beetles, spiders, snakes, and possums may escape attack by pretending to be dead. This is called death-feigning. When a predator is near, the prey will become very, very still over a period of time that can last from minutes to hours. For example, hognosed snakes play dead by rolling on their backs with their mouths open, simulating the slackness of death.

pretending to be dead

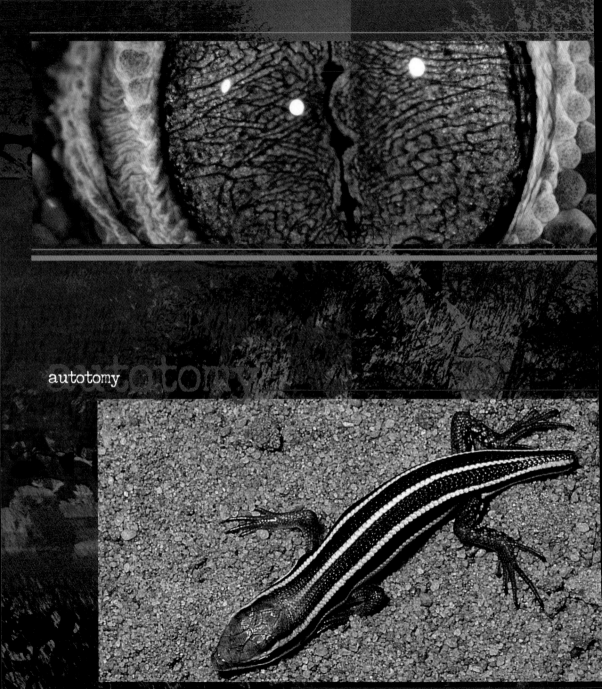

autotomy

If caught, many lizards are prepared to sacrifice parts of their bodies to save themselves. This strategy is called autotomy. Special parts of the vertebrae in the lizard's tail allow it to shed off its tail and run away, leaving the twitching wormlike part behind. A new tail will grow in its place, but it is less impressive than the original.

Clarify!

sacrifice

a, b, or c ?

a lose

b give up for something more valuable

c donate

Chemical deterrents are useful for defense, too. Some insects have harmful chemicals stored in sacs in their bodies. They squirt out these chemicals onto their attacker. The chemicals can be squirted out at up to 500 spurts a second.

Synonym: A word or term that has the same meaning as another word or term

deterrents
Which is the correct synonym: a, b, or c?

a discouragements

b ingredients

c liquids made from oil

Categories of Interesting Defenses

looking bigger than normal size	toads and bullfrogs
feigning death	?
sacrificing body parts	?
chemical deterrents	insect

Communal Defense

Predict: What do you think this chapter will be about?

Many animals work cooperatively to protect themselves from predators. The spotted hyenas that hunt the herds of eland are frequently defeated by the cooperative strategies used by the herd. They rarely manage to kill.

As well as using physical horns and hooves to protect themselves against the predatory hyenas, a herd will take a group action to defend itself. The cow eland and the young calves will stay well back from the attackers, and the cows without calves will move forward in defense.

Strategies

When pursued, oxen will form a defensive ring. With their massive horns pointing outward and the cows and calves in the ring's center, the oxen can usually defeat an attack.

The benefits of cooperative defense strategies have positive results for survival.

Flocks, shoals, and herds, or dense groups, can often distract or confuse a predator. Lapwings will join forces to drive away crows, which come near their nesting sites to prey on their eggs. In colonies of some leaf cutter ants, large worker ants cut leaf segments and carry them back to the nest as food for the fungi gardens that they grow. In this task, the worker ants are very susceptible to attacks by wasps because their jaws are occupied, so they are accompanied by smaller worker ants. These small ants have the job of attacking the wasps.

Communal Defense Strategies

Key points	Interesting Facts
Animals work together cooperatively.	Animals use • physical strategies • defense rings • distraction
Elands use horns and hooves to protect themselves.	Leaf cutter ants are very susceptible to attacks by wasps when their jaws are occupied.

Are these in the right category?
What do you think?

Index

Making connections — What connections can
you make to the elements of protecting self
and community in *Action Defense*?

facing threats

cooperation

protecting
family

adapting

bluff ← Text-to-Self

mimicking

working as
a team

security

defense

body protection

Text-to-text

Talk about other texts you may have read that have similar features. Compare the texts.

Text-to-world

Talk about situations in the world that might connect to elements in the text.

Planning an
Informational Explanation

Select a topic that explains how or why something is the way it is or how something works.

↓

Make a mind map of questions about the topic.

Action Defense

In what ways do animals protect themselves?

How do animals use camouflage?

Which interesting or unusual defenses are used?

How can animals evade attack?

How do animals threaten or bluff their predators?

How do animals cooperate to protect each other?

↓

Locate the information that you need.

library   Internet   experts

You can... Organize your information by using the questions you selected as headings.

Make a Plan

a   Strategies

d   Flight from attack

b   Camouflages

e   Interesting defenses

c   Withdrawal, threat, and bluff

f   Communal defense strategies

You can... design some visuals to include in your report. You can use graphs, diagrams, labels, charts, tables, cross-sections.

An Informational Explanation

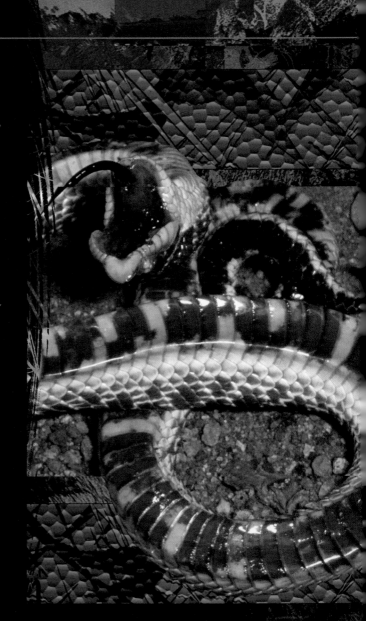

- Explores causes and effects

- Uses scientific/ technical vocabulary

- Uses present tense

- Is written in a formal style that is concise and accurate

- Avoids author opinion